Abilene**InSight**

Jan Wilson

essay by Lori Brack

Arts Council of Dickinson County,
Abilene, Kansas

Abilene**InSight**

The exhibition Abilene Insight was organized by the Arts Council of Dickinson County, Abilene, Kansas.

Editor: Lori Brack.

For information regarding this project, write or call the publisher:
Arts Council of Dickinson County
Box 604
Abilene, Kansas 67410
(785) 263-1884

Library of Congress Catalog Card Number: 99-73528
ISBN: 0-9672517-0-2

Printed in the United States by Mennonite Press Inc., Newton, Kansas

Supporters for publication and exhibition projects:
Wichita Greyhound Charities, Inc.
Arts Council of Dickinson County
Kansas Arts Commission
Lorraine McClain, American Express Financial Advisors
City of Abilene
Holm Automotive Center
USD 435

This program is presented in part by the Kansas Arts Commission, a state agency, and the National Endowment for the Arts, a federal agency.

Dedicated to the life and spirit of Stan Martin

Contents

Acknowledgements

Many people offered enthusiastic support and advice to *Abilene InSight*. This book would not have happened without the foresight and vigilance of the Arts Council of Dickinson County and its members. The Arts Council continues to provide enrichment through the arts for the Abilene community. Victoria Martin, director, and Gwyn Johnson, associate director, allowed me the freedom to work in a way which was personally and artistically satisfying. They were passionate agents for the whole process.

Thank you to the Wichita Greyhound Charities, Inc. for its generous support for this book. Additional underwriters for the book project and the artist-in-residence program are the Kansas Arts Commission, Lorraine McClain, American Express Financial Advisors, City of Abilene, Holm Automotive Center, and USD 435.

I feel very privileged to have worked with the students and staff of Abilene High School on the accompanying "Working" project. Abilene residents are fortunate to have such bright and competent young people in their community. These kids dedicated so much time, talent, and energy to the project in their already hectic schedules. I am grateful for their contributions. The "Working" project would not have happened without journalism and English teacher Carol Stephens. She contributed her own time and always thought of her students first. Thanks also to English teacher Ginger Ireton for incorporating the writing portion of the project into her curriculum. She allowed students freedom to speak with their own voices. I salute Myron Graber, high school principal, and Jim Lambert, superintendent of schools, for going to bat for "Working" when there was uncertainty about whether it could happen. They supported this hands-on approach in multiple disciplines as a valuable educational experience to prepare young people for future challenges. Thanks also goes to photojournalist Tom Dorsey and graphic artist Pam Harris, both of Salina, for sharing their expertise with the "Working" group. Special thanks to Lori Brack for her wisdom and words. Her talent made this a richer project for me.

My warmest appreciation goes to the people I photographed for this exhibition and book. Thank you for allowing me to step into your lives for just a moment. I appreciate being allowed to include each image with all the others to form this sense of community.

A continuing debt of gratitude goes to the people at the Salina Art Center and to Terry Evans for ongoing artistic inspiration and encouragement. Above all, I extend my appreciation to Tom, Chris and Jeff for their love and patience. They literally waded through this project as it took shape and consumed our home for many months.

Jan Wilson

Artist Statement

These photographs were made in the Abilene community from May 1997 to May 1999, where I spent my time on the streets, in businesses, in homes and in schools. The sixty portraits represent an earnest look at the people I encountered in these places. This is not intended to provide definitive documentation of what went on in Abilene from 1997 to 1999, but rather a glimpse into some parts of daily life in this place. I photographed each person one at a time. I printed each photograph one at a time. I framed each portrait one at a time. But once the group is hung in a room or gathered in a book and can be viewed together, they become a celebration of community.

I set my camera's sights on Abilene as a place to live, work and play. It is a multidimensional place which sees itself as a town with a history descending from the Wild West, the proud home of a national hero, the center of an agricultural and commercial area, a regional employment magnet, a growing site of light industry, and a place where the arts hold importance.

Photographs have a lingering power. They can fix a moment. They can help us embrace our history – personal or communal. The photographic portrait tradition, in many cases, consists of facing the camera, smiling, and trying for a flattering result. I tried to go beyond that and to approach these people as they are. I was interested in the immediacy of an unguarded moment.

These subjects expressed to me a rare and comfortable naturalness. I saw the joy of eating watermelon on a hot summer day, the fun of a free-spirited ride with grandma on a merry-go-round, or the relaxation of a stolen moment during the workday. My subjects engaged the camera with a strong sense of dignity or curiosity. Sometimes they paid me the compliment of ignoring me as I – and they – worked. Their environments often helped define the subject, but the focus always stayed with some aspect of the individual. I have great respect for the people in these pictures. They allowed me to enter their worlds and to see them in some authentic way. I enjoyed the interaction between the subjects and me, the picture-taker. After an intense project like this in Abilene, people have now become a vital part of my work as an artist.

A companion exhibition called "Working" put me in touch with a group of Abilene High School students. The project was a photographic and journalistic look by students at themselves as they approached the complicated mix of employment, school obligations and the challenges of their teen years. As a group, they were very skilled at "seeing." They used a variety of points-of-view to explore working from its necessity, to drudgery, to preparing for the future. I am always amazed at the fresh approach young eyes can bring to a subject.

Jan Wilson

Abilene**InSight**

by Lori Brack

"Town neighbors are different from country neighbors. You get to know them faster in the country."

In Abilene, Kansas, people still take care of each other.

At Bankes Drug Store downtown on a sunny February afternoon, I mentioned to the woman behind the soda fountain that I needed a glass of water and a place to sit to get rid of a headache.

"The pressure's changing," she told me. "Lots of headaches going around today."

On one trip by the booth where I sat, she dropped off two cherry candies. "These may help – no medication to them; they'll just coat your throat," she said.

By the third glass of water and the candies, I was feeling human enough to notice a mail carrier, finished with his route, slide onto a stool at the fountain and unfold the daily paper. A little boy and his aunt in the first booth ordered two small Sailors – a traditional local treat usually made with chocolate ice cream and marshmallow topping.

Nolan, the little boy, said he was four, and his Aunt Marsha prompted him to tell me about his preschool field trip two days earlier.

"Where did you go?" I asked.

Nolan, struggling to swallow a spoonful of ice cream, hadn't spoken when a voice from behind us announced, "The post office!"

The mail carrier, of course.

Abilene reveals its character that way – one conversation at a time, one face at a time. People call this north-central Kansas town of about 6,500, "a good place to visit *and* a good place to live."

Abilene sells itself as a visitor attraction based in "history, heroes, and hospitality." Appearances matter in a local economy boosted each summer by tourists seeking traces of the Old West or memories of a president. A drive through town offers plenty of the picturesque: Victorian mansions, cowboy souvenir shops, and rolling lawns surrounding the

1. Central Kansas Free Fair Parade Crowd, August 1997

"We're all grandmothers having a ball!"

Eisenhower complex. Buckeye Avenue, a visitor's first impression, is home to fast food joints and signs indicating tourist attractions. Downtown still offers that drug store soda fountain and a locally owned jewelry store where you can get a watch fixed right on the premises. Residential streets marked NW and NE retain in their structures one hundred years of Abilene's history.

In this town, a visitor can drive up an ordinary street lined with houses, only to be suddenly submerged in the deep shadow of grain elevators emerging from the ground like monuments. The real statues in town, like an eleven-foot statue of Dwight D. Eisenhower or life-size bronze greyhounds, shrink in comparison.

Pictures of Abilene's economy and history have been made before. Jan Wilson's photographs of Abilene – images of faces and forms – exist because she got out of the car and walked into people's lives, where she stayed long enough to find the truth in things like coffee breaks, parades, and cutting hair. If her eloquent photographs could speak with human voices, maybe they would say a few of the things Abilene told me on a single day when I was audacious enough to think that I could capture a whole community in the voices of fifteen of its people. Without exception, I was invited into the homes and lives of these people and more who were happy – even eager – to talk about and demonstrate their pastimes, concerns and pride.

Over coffee in a warm kitchen with women in their 70s, standing in an antique store with the owner, or sitting in the parlor of a Heritage Home with a high school junior, three things kept bobbing to the surface:

Abilene loves to celebrate its heritage; Abilene takes care of its children; and Abilene is a safe place to live.

Even the ex-mayor agreed.

"We don't want to think we're in a shell," said John Zutavern as he and Ralph Reese settled down for coffee. "Abilene is doing business internationally. We have a lot of tourist attractions. It's just the quality of life."

The men also point to the lower cost of living and stability in local politics. Business is good in Abilene. Owners of Frenchie's Barber Shop,

Reese Jewelry and Prairie Antiques all agreed: With loyal local trade and the summer tourist season, you can make a living in Abilene. And you can learn a lot, too.

B.G. French (that's Beverly Gordon, but he says nobody ever calls him that) has been cutting hair in Abilene for forty-two years. "You hear how many divorces are going on, who's got medical problems," he said from his ballcap-festooned one-chair barber shop on North Cedar. "They want to tell somebody and they got me where I got to listen. Sometimes I don't remember when they get out the door."

Beside his skill at discretion, or maybe because of it, French boasts at least one famous friend. He displays photographs of Abilene favorite son Marlin Fitzwater above the shop's mirror. Each is inscribed to "Frenchie," and picture the former presidential press secretary in various official poses with presidents Reagan and Bush.

"Abilene's a good place to live. It's laid back. Nobody's rushing here and there," Frenchie said. "Now, I get grown men coming in here with their kids, and I used to cut their hair up here on the board." He gestured to the barber chair where little boys – for decades – have crawled up onto a board laid across the chair's arms to raise them high enough for a trim.

After they grow up and grow older, lots of local folk "retire" to Abilene. Lynda Alstrom, owner of Prairie Antiques, returned to Abilene from Oklahoma with her husband after fifteen and a half years. During the summers, Alstrom promotes Abilene's lifestyle as a guide for the Convention and Visitors Bureau's historical van tours. "I'm asked over and over again: 'Why is there no graffiti on your buildings and bridges?' I tell them, 'We will not tolerate it.' Then they tell me that if they decide to relocate, they're going to look at our town."

Lifelong farmer Lee Hoffman and his wife Edna moved into town in May 1998 after working a farm on Daisy Road for sixty years. On Valentine's Day 1999, the couple celebrated their sixty-fifth wedding anniversary. "We had a big man. That's why he tied the knot so good," Mr. Hoffman said. "The minister was six foot seven!"

"I close up when it's nice and play golf. My customers will be back. They know where I am."

"You come to Abilene and there's a lot of hospitality. People are very nice to you. I would say some of the time it's boring, but sometimes really exciting."

The Hoffmans were often involved in Abilene institutions and projects. Mrs. Hoffman did Gray Lady work at the hospital for twenty years, and Mr. Hoffman still helps at Heritage Day with the antique carousel, one of Abilene's treasured national landmarks. After the couple's fiftieth anniversary, Mr. Hoffman bought an autoharp and he now entertains at local and area nursing homes, birthday parties, and senior citizens' activities with old-fashioned songs and hymns.

"I feel safe here. This is a good community," Mrs. Hoffman said.

So good that people downtown boasted they leave their cars unlocked. And safe enough that even high school students remark on it.

"There's not very much crime," Amanda Riffel told me as we sat in the parlor of her home on NE Seventh. "You know everybody around you." A wall full of framed pictures of her home's past residents watched over our conversation. Here I learned about the holiday Heritage Home tours, and about the compelling photograph of Amanda at 16 sitting on the floor of her room:

"The photographer was going through Heritage Homes and she saw me there and she said, 'Don't move. I want to take your picture.' So she went to get her camera. I was just sitting there; I don't know why."

That may have been the last time Amanda found the leisure just to sit. After school, she works at Mr. K's Express, a fast-food store, where she makes Twisters ("They're like a Blizzard," she said), takes piano lessons, and participates in FFA, German Club, and 4H. As if that wasn't enough, Amanda, who will graduate as a member of the class of 2000, competes in the shot put in track. High school sports are "very big – very, *very* big" for fans of all ages in Abilene, and she believes in supporting the teams, win or lose. Off times might find her "cruising Buckeye" with friends, turning around at McDonald's or Dairy Queen at one end, and downtown on Third, past "cement park" at the other.

Teenagers aren't the only ones who find entertainment on the streets of Abilene. Tom and Lupe Garcia have lived in their house on NW Third for thirty-one years, and enjoy their front-row seats for the town's annual Central Kansas Free Fair parade. Tom said you can't find a place on the family's deep and shady front porch unless you get there plenty early on the day of the parade. He chuckled at memories of entertaining parade-watchers over the years.

"I think it's a good town," he said of Abilene. "We never had any trouble here." The couple raised seven children in Abilene, and most of them still live in Kansas, three of them in Abilene.

"I don't think we can fit all of us in one house," Lupe said.

What fits into one house? Into one town? Can any set of walls hold the meaning of community?

If not, the 100-year-old home where Dorothy Taylor and her husband Dale live came pretty close. It is home not only to the couple, but to an ever-growing collection of dolls and stuffed animals. Dorothy Taylor offers visitors their choice from a box and chair filled with toys. She smiles most of the time and talks about the good times and good friends she has made in Abilene.

"We all think a lot of each other," she said of her friends Velma McConkey and Dorothy Barber, who stopped by Taylor's house for coffee and to fill me in on Abilene's religious, social, and historical life.

"This whole town is my family," Dorothy Barber said. After growing up in Abilene, Barber left for 37 years, but she didn't think twice about where to settle after retirement. She has never regretted that decision.

Here I heard more about the ways Abilene celebrates its heritage – like Chisholm Trail Day and the Central Kansas Free Fair parade, which plays a big part in the lives of these women, too. A couple of years ago Velma investigated the fair theme, "From Trails to Rails," and created two large Kansas maps which she attached to the sides of a bus. Dorothy Taylor rode in the parade with Velma on a flatbed trailer. Both were soaked by the rain which fell that August day; the photograph of the pair shows them holding umbrellas and wrapped in sheets of plastic.

"She looked like a bride under her umbrella," Dorothy Taylor said of Velma. "And I had on dark so I could have been the gentleman!" She laughed at her interpretation of the photograph, and then pulled out a print of the picture to show me.

"All the churches get along beautiful. We think that heaven's going to have some of all of us in it."

These are the kind of women whose exuberance spilled over into invitations in the mail to join them for Abilene's annual Lenten Luncheons. They assured me that the whole town shows up and that the food is always good. The three women have taught Sunday School and lament the dwindling attendance of young people at church. Although it has been years since any of their children were students in Abilene schools, they keep an eye on football, basketball and wrestling. When something is going right, they want to make sure the person responsible hears about it.

"They've really got a wrestling program here," Velma said. "I've got to call the coach and tell him how good he's doing." She looked to her friends as though to prompt them to remind her to do just that.

Community as culture and geography, mutual concerns and interdependence, requires people who participate and who care. Here is community – three retired women around a kitchen table talking about their lives. One of them held her pet poodle wearing a T-shirt with "Killer" emblazoned in glitter on the back. Another wore a glove to ease the throbbing in her swollen hand, injured in a fall earlier in the year. Her handiwork was evident in the necklace she presented me as I left. The third wouldn't allow the conversation to break up until she had given me a toy collie dog from her collection, and marked this meeting by taking photographs of us standing in her kitchen. Here, with these women who share friendships forged through years of church, child-raising, and work, I found Abilene—the kind of place where people let you in.

The Photographs

2. Katie Miller: After Dancing in Her Front Yard, May 1997

3. Lee Hoffman: Cutting Boards from Trees He Planted in 1938, October 1997

4. Jessica Burchard and Tanya Marshall: Mud Volleyball Pit, Fourth of July 1997

5. Jill Angst: Watermelon Eating Contest, Fourth of July 1997

6. Drew Needham: Mud Volleyball, Fourth of July 1997

7. Jenny Sare, Nikki Withrow and Team Members: Mud Volleyball, Fourth of July 1997

8. Dalton Weaver & Turtle: Turtle Races, Fourth of July 1997

9. Kip Racy, Shawn Lemon: Three-on-Three Basketball, Fourth of July 1997

10. Robert Kohman: Delivering Wheat to ADM, Fourth of July 1997

11. Corey Casteel: ADM Milling, Fourth of July 1997

12. Caitlin and Wanda Sullivan, Alexis Lawson, and Dylan Sullivan: Sullivan's Garage Sale, May 1999

13. Amanda Riffel: Heritage Homes Christmas Tour, December 1997

14. Cathy Strowig and Betty Strowig: Plaza Theatre, March 1998

15. Michelle Meade and Richard Esvang: Great Plains Theatre Festival, February 1998

16. Maureen Morton: In Her Garden, June 1997

17. Nick Glanzer: Driveway Basketball Game, December 1997

18. David Zey: Zey's Market, October 1997

19. Marcene Fowler and Anne Robson: Daily Bike Ride, November 1997

20. Lucas Geske and Keenan Cole: Delivering The Abilene Reflector-Chronicle, August 1997

21. Fay Johnson and Gwyn Johnson: Sand Hills West of Abilene, March 1998

22. Randall Bathurst: Burning Wheat Stubble, July 1997

23. Randy and Melvin Leckron: Listening To the Truck Radio, April 1999

24. Molly Whitehair: Abilene High School Homecoming, September 1997

25. Mandy Ramey: Abilene High School Homecoming, September 1997

26. Jamye Jo Taplin, Emily Wyatt, and Jessica Barker: Abilene High School Homecoming, September 1997

27. Jim Turner: Third and Vine Streets, October 1997

28. Wendell Gugler, Jack Royer, John Zutavern and Ralph Reese's Coffee Cup: Bankes Drug Store, February 1998

29. Merle Vahsholtz: On the Porch of the Vahsholtz Mansion, May 1999

30. Inga Bow: Bow Studio & Gallery, February 1998

31. Team Ropers: Hickok Days Team Roping Competition, May 1999

32. Jessie Rock: Central Kansas Free Fair, August 1997

33. Justin Cook: Central Kansas Free Fair, August 1997

34. Chris Bowers: Diverting Traffic at Central Kansas Free Fair Parade, August 1997

35. Dorothy Taylor and Velma McConkey: Central Kansas Free Fair Parade, August 1997

36. Kristina Montgomery: Russell Stover Candies Inc., August 1997

37. Helen Clegg: Brown Memorial Home Kitchen, September 1997

38. William (Sonny) Davis: Buckeye Avenue, May 1997

39. Larry Crawford, Richard Vaughn: National Greyhound Association Annual Meeting Races, April 1999

40. Patrick Woodcox: Cedar Street, November 1997

41. Tom and Lupe Garcia: Daily Walk Near Eisenhower Park, May 1997

42. John Hansen: Eisenhower Boyhood Home, May 1997

43. Ralph Thomas: Abilene & Smoky Valley Railroad Association, April 1999

44. B.G. French: Frenchie's Barber Shop, July 1997

45. David McClain: Washing Windows, August 1997

46. Brian Moon: Great Plains Manufacturing Inc., October 1997

47. Linda Diehl: EBC Broadcasting Office, July 1997

48. Don Hedleston: ALCO Warehouse Security, June 1997

49. Mike Pantano: Holm Automotive Body Shop, September 1997

50. Tony Stejskal: Western Resources, July 1997

51. Jason Schuber: Holm Automotive Center Body Shop, September 1997

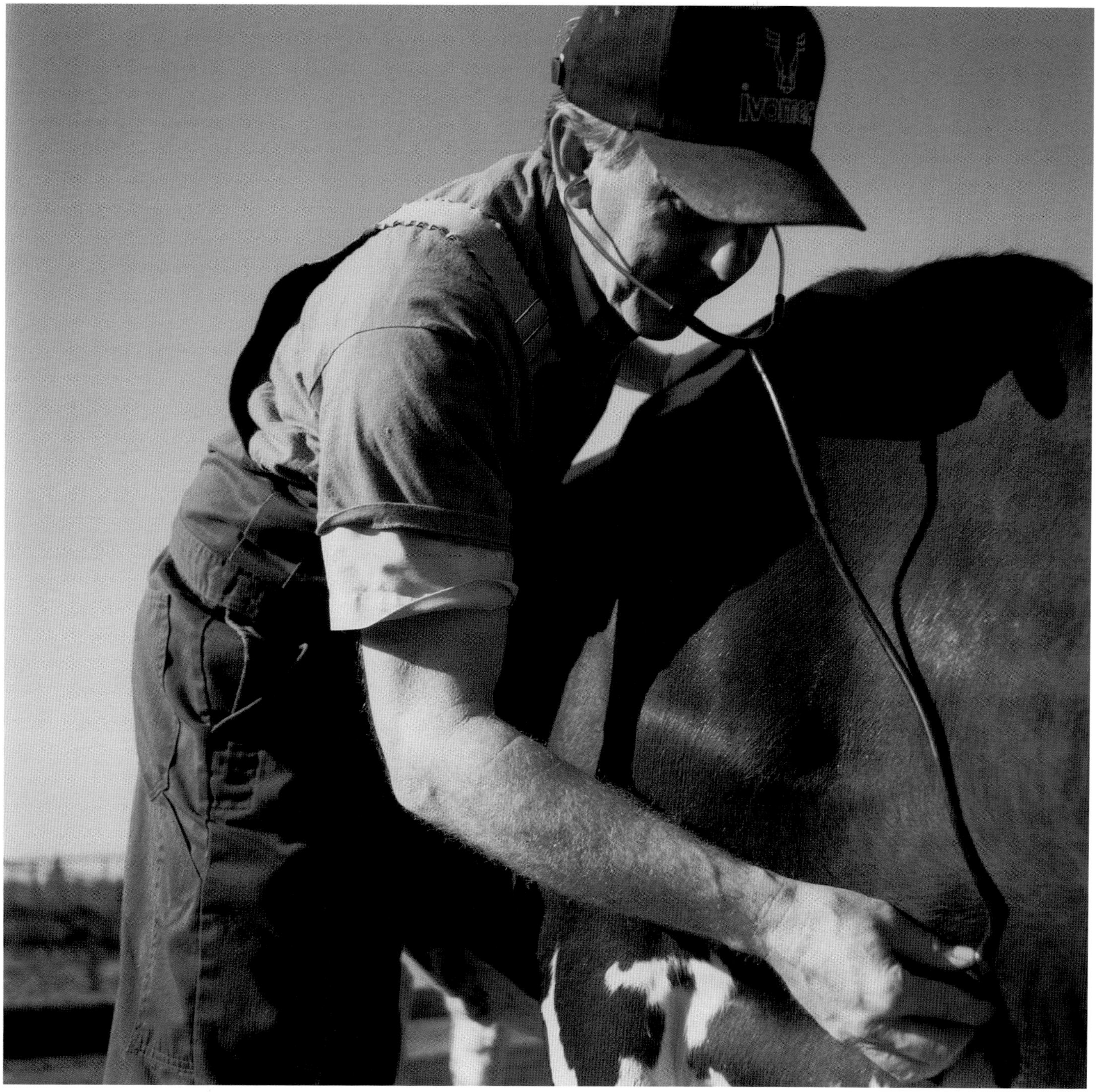

52. Dr. Mike Whitehair: Diagnosing Displacement of the Abomasum, April 1999

53. Brown Memorial Home Residents and Staff, April 1999

54. "Daisy and Rose" – Ann Manning and Jessie Polzella: Chisholm Trail Day, October 1997

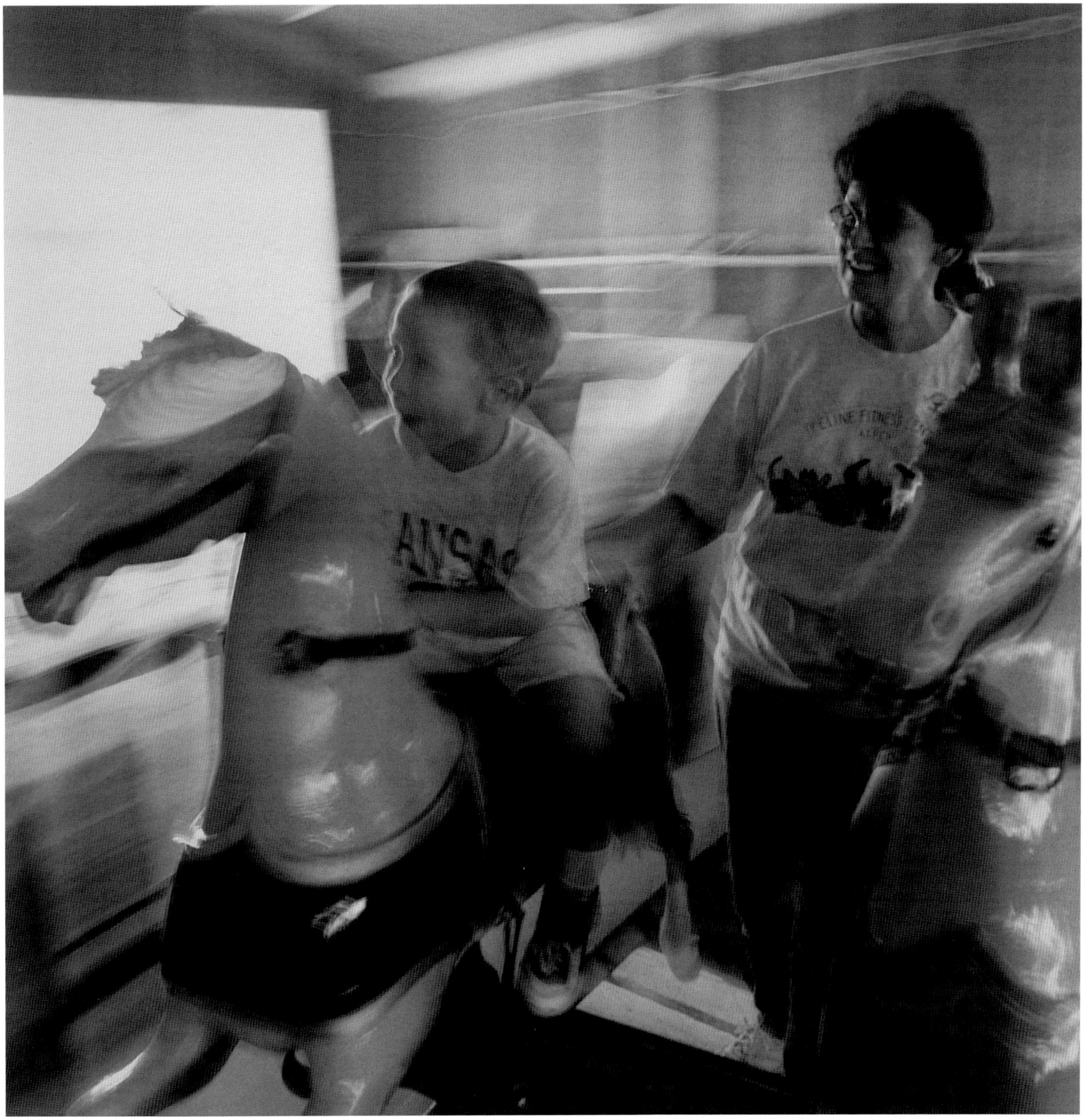

55. Ramey and Cindy Harwood: 1901 C.W. Parker Carousel, Heritage Center, October 1997

56. "Two Paws" Ottensmeier and "Fox Running" Peterson: Chisholm Trail Day, October 1997

57. Deb and Madison Roth: In Their Home, February 1998

58. Lynda Alstrom: Annual City-Wide Sidewalk Sale, May 1999

59. Gabriel and Tim Johnson, Bernice Peterson, and Dennis Medina: Daylight Donuts, April 1998

60. Ty Martin, Kirk Rose, Ryan Carver, Matthew Riffel: Cement Park, May 1999

Notes on the Photographs

1, 32, 33, 34, 35. The Central Kansas Free Fair and Parade are the center of rural community activities for the year. Traffic is diverted and the parade runs down Buckeye Avenue to Third Street, then on to the fairgrounds. People camp out ahead of time to get their favorite viewing spots. On the day of the parade in August 1997, it poured rain in Salina where I live. I drove to Abilene thinking the parade would be canceled, or maybe that it would not be raining there. It was a downpour in Abilene, and regardless of weather, the parade always goes on. The event also includes a carnival, and the fair is the culmination of 4-H projects for the year. Prize winners at the fair go on to compete in the Kansas State Fair in Hutchinson.

2. This portrait was taken on the first day I photographed in Abilene. As I drove down the street, I saw a little girl dancing in her yard. She had choreographed a lovely ballet and was joyously expressing herself. As soon as she noticed my presence the dancing stopped, but she shyly allowed me to take her photograph standing in shadow in her doorway.

3. This photograph was taken on Chisholm Trail Day where old-time ways of doing things are demonstrated. Lee Hoffman brought trees that he had planted on his farm in 1938. The trees were used to demonstrate how to make lumber. You can see in his glasses a reflection of the boards in the back of his pickup truck.

4, 5, 6, 7, 8, 9. These activities are part of the city's Fourth of July celebration which culminates in a fireworks display. In the mud volleyball games, the dirtier a player gets, the more exciting it is. I positioned myself near the net and in one heroic dive for a spike, a player sent a huge wave of mud washing over me. My camera and my clothes were covered with mud, but I got the shot. I was glad I caught the two girls partially submerged in mud because the photograph still shows the contrast between clean and dirty. City firefighters have a hose ready for clean-up after the games. Turtle races, the watermelon eating contest, and three-on-three basketball provide activities for everyone.

10, 11. When the wheat is ripe, the lives of farmers and their families revolve around getting it cut and hauled to the grain elevator. It is a hectic time. Robert Kohman, a high school student, is driving a load of wheat to the elevator on the Fourth of July, and Corey Casteel's job is to make sure every bit of wheat gets out of the truck and into the catch basin. This was the same day the town kids were playing mud volleyball, but someone at the elevator said, "I don't mind. The wheat won't wait. I can have fun after harvest."

13. At the annual Heritage Homes tour, residents are stationed around their homes to impart information about the history of the houses. When I walked into this room, Amanda Riffel was sitting in this position. She had grown weary of being a tour guide and had gone off to the corner to take a break.

Glenn Bowers: The Fitness Center, April 1999. The Fitness Center is a new workout facility in what was once a grocery store. It is managed by Memorial Hospital.

14. This theatre started as the Bonebrake Opera House in 1879, and then became the Seelye Opera House in 1900. The first movies were shown in 1905. Homer Strowig redesigned the theatre in 1936 in the Art Deco style. As the Plaza Theatre, it was the site of Dwight Eisenhower's press conference to announce his candidacy for president in 1952. Three movie world premiers have taken place here. It showed first-run movies and was a popular gathering place, especially for young people, and was one of only eight independent theatres in Kansas. Cathy and Betty Strowig, Homer's granddaughter and daughter-in-law respectively, say it was often an economic struggle to operate the theatre, but they were dedicated to providing a valuable service to the community. On May 30, 1999, as I was ready to publish this book, rain from a severe thunderstorm caused the collapse of the west wall of the building, requiring the demolition of this extraordinary place.

15. Michelle Meade and Richard Esvang were actors doing stage and commercial work in New York City when friends in Abilene convinced them to relocate. They opened The Great Plains Theatre Festival, a professional regional theatre. It brings in professional actors from across the nation, and also uses local talent in productions. The theatre, a converted church building, offers a year-round schedule of plays, classes, and live literature.

16. Many times during this project I would drive around Abilene without an agenda. One day, as I drove down Northeast Tenth Street, Maureen Morton tending her garden caught my eye. She was positioned inside this beautiful little lattice gateway which acted as a picture frame.

17. By adjusting the height of the goal, Nick Glanzer can feel like a seven-foot tall professional basketball player dunking the ball.

18. The Zey family has operated this neighborhood grocery store for three generations. Louis Zey bought the store in 1928 by trading his wife Pearl's new living room furniture for the business. (She never got over it, the family says.) The business was not profitable until Louis bought Pearl an ice cream maker. She would hand crank five gallons of ice cream at a time and sell two dips for a nickel. Louis was the promoter, while Pearl got things done.

19. These women ride eight miles every day.

20. The Abilene Reflector-Chronicle is an evening paper, so kids can still be employed as deliverers. These boys were substituting for a friend on his daily route.

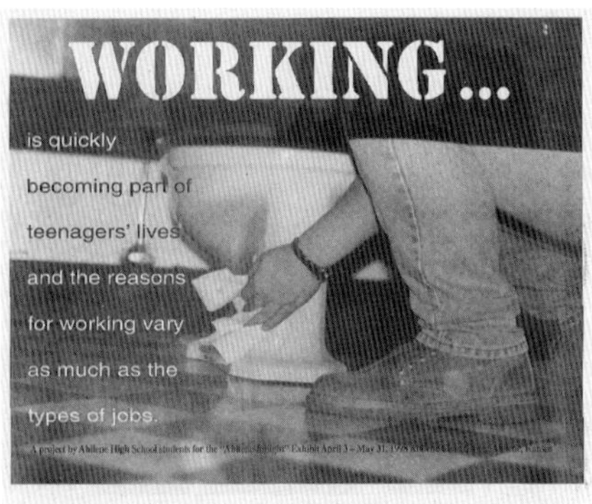

WORKING...

is quickly becoming part of teenagers' lives and the reasons for working vary as much as the types of jobs.

As part of the Artist-In-Residence program, Jan Wilson worked with students at Abilene High School. They produced an eight-page newspaper on the subject of teenagers and employment called "Working."

21. Gwyn Johnson from Arkansas and Fay Johnson from Long Island, N.Y., are transplants to Abilene who fell in love with the prairie. They have long studied and gathered prairie grasses and forbs. This bunch contains the "Big Three" tallgrass prairie grasses: Big Bluestem, Indian Grass, and Switch Grass. Abilene is located in the midgrass prairie, and on the edge of the tallgrass prairie to the east. Short grasses are found throughout western Kansas and the high plains.

22. I was finished for the day and on my way out of Abilene when I saw smoke in the sky. I knew it was the time of year for burning wheat stubble, so I followed the smoke in order to photograph the flames for another project. When I got to the burning field my camera was out of film, and by the time I loaded new film the flames were racing far across the field. Randall Bathurst was tending the fire, so I made him the subject, and the flames, smoke and dirt became the backdrop.

23, 52. Randy and Melvin Leckron are father-and-son farmers who run a busy milking operation, 500 feet of which is located within city limits. Their day came to a halt when fourth-grader Sarah, Randy's daughter, was on the radio to read her report on "Willy Wonka and the Chocolate Factory." Then they returned to the matter of a sick cow. Dr. Whitehair found a "twisted stomach," and the cow was sent to market. After observing the techniques the veterinarian used, I was glad I was a photographer because I did not want to go where he had to go to make the diagnosis.

24, 25, 26. The homecoming football game is an exciting time. Crowning a homecoming queen – Molly Whitehair in this photograph – is a long-standing tradition in high school. The three girls watching the game reminded me of three important aspects of childhood – dreaming, impish exuberance, and sweet innocence. To capture the enthusiasm of the cheerleader, I used a slow shutter speed and then fired a flash.

27. On this day, I had one of the high school students from the "Working" project with me. We were talking about looking for opportunities when we drove by a man weighing rocks with a scale on the bank of a dry river. I talked to the student about point of view and why I selected a wide angle lens. I got down on one knee to look up at him. This gives him a monumental look. Dorothea Lange, who photographed during the Depression, often used this point of view. She said it gave her subjects dignity.

28. At three o'clock in the afternoon, you can find these men at Bankes Drug Store downtown to discuss the events of the day. Ralph Reese is not pictured because he quickly finished his coffee and went back to work at his jewelry store just down the street.

29. Merle Vahsholtz's home is the "oldest, most historic, and only certified tour house in Kansas," she says. Merle and her husband bought it in 1974 after it had been abandoned for two years. It took one hundred people and five years to restore the Victorian mansion. She asked not to have her coffee cup in this picture, but I was taking too much time and her coffee was getting cold.

30. This is a busy working studio, but I chose to focus on the artist and her art.

31. Hickok Days run for two days in May. The Bulls and Barrels event happens on Friday night, and Saturday there is team roping. Two riders lasso a steer, one at the head and the other at the hind legs. It is a timed competition. Chinks and roper's chaps were among the prizes donated by Gerald Roberts, a champion rodeo cowboy who lives in Abilene.

36. Kristina Montgomery, an employee at Russell Stover Candies Inc., is hand dipping chocolate-covered cherries in the factory's public demonstration area. The candy plant is an example of new industry which has helped to make Abilene a regional employment center.

37. I enjoy cooking. I like the things found in kitchens – stoves, utensils, pots and pans. Even in the gleaming shininess of an industrial kitchen, Helen Clegg seems pretty comfortable.

Student photographers from the "Working" project were (standing) Wendy Lagrasso, Allyson Crumpton, Christiana Cooper, Toshia Bezdeck, Larissa Paulson, Kelli Regier, Richard Green, Amanda Dutton, Kelli Verble, (kneeling) Rachael King, Cynthia Bowley, and Megan Barbur.

38. American flags line the main streets of Abilene. They are part of the way the town celebrates its place in American history, and give the town a festive, patriotic look. Not only did President Dwight D. Eisenhower spent his boyhood here, but historic figures like Wild Bill Hickok once lived in Abilene. From 1867 to 1871, cattle were driven from Texas to Abilene along the Chisholm Trail to catch the railroad to go to slaughter in Chicago or New York. The United Telephone Company, which became Sprint Corporation, was started in Abilene by Cleyson L. Brown. Beta Sigma Phi social sorority was founded here. Marlin Fitzwater, press secretary to presidents Ronald Reagan and George Bush, was raised here.

39. Dickinson County has been called the "Greyhound Capital of the World" because of the number of greyhounds raised in the area. Abilene is the home of the National Greyhound Association. Twice a year, dog owners from across the nation gather in Abilene for meetings and racing competitions. Greyhounds usually race at parimutuel tracks, but at the annual meeting there is no gambling – just spirited competition. It is a time for owners to showcase and sell dogs.

40. City worker Patrick Woodcox is fixing a broken water main on Cedar Street. He was standing in a huge hole. A couple of days later I drove by, and the hole was only a tiny patched place in the street. I could barely tell it had been opened up. During months of photographing, I ran into Patrick several times as he worked on projects around Abilene.

42. I chose to focus on one person at The Eisenhower Center rather than to make a vista shot of the grounds with people in it. The Eisenhower Library and Museum attracts tourists, school field trips, scholars doing research, and international visitors.

43. The Abilene & Smoky Valley Railroad Association is staffed mostly by volunteers. Many of these people once worked for the railroads. The association runs an excursion train that takes groups from the Buckeye Avenue Station to Enterprise, Kansas, five miles away. Passengers include the general public, school groups, adult dinner groups, and Scout troops. I found myself putting down the camera to just enjoy the ride.

44. Frenchie's Barber Shop is a small place, so there is a lot of information about Frenchie in this shot – his baseball cap collection, photos connecting him to notable people, golf trinkets, tools of barbering, and business papers.

45. David McClain is a middle school teacher. During the summer, he and his daughter, Sarah, and son, Sam, run a window-washing business.

46. Photographing inside Great Plains Manufacturing was a challenge. It was dark, so I let light from the welding arc create lines in the photograph. I had no idea of the identity of the person inside the welding mask. When I went to the manager of the plant I said, "I'm sure there's no way you can identify this welder," but he immediately answered, "Oh sure. That's Brian Moon."

47. EBC Broadcasting offices are housed in an old bank. Linda Diehl's office was in this windowless bank vault.

48. Don Hedleston lives in Wakefield. Job opportunties draw people from surrounding towns to Abilene. The ALCO Stores can be traced back to the Racket Store (1901). The Duckwall family from Abilene later opened the Duckwall Five and Dime Stores in many small communities. When the retail market changed to include discount stores, A.L. Duckwall opened ALCO Discount Stores in 1968. There were 97 Duckwall stores in eleven states still operating in 1999, and 169 ALCO stores in nineteen states.

49. After I took this photograph of Mike Pantano, I was not sure I got the shot right, so I asked him to pull the seal a little bit more, and then again and again so I could get the right exposure. By the time I left he was pretty exhausted.

50. This shot reminded me of how valuable a UV filter is in protecting a camera lens. The filter was damaged by sparks, but my lens was OK.

51. The lights in the background harden the paint on freshly painted cars after body work is done. This is a very clean area and it had a feeling of white-on-white with the black line of the paint sprayer running through it.

53. The Brown Memorial Home was built by Cleyson L. Brown in 1928, and dedicated to the memory of Jacob and Mary Brown by their children. The home for senior citizens was envisioned by Brown as a way to provide housing and social activities for the elderly at a low cost. The home is funded by the Brown Memorial Foundation, and accepts contributions toward its work. Brown Memorial Home residents and staff in April 1999 were Marilyn Palmer, Margie Picking, Mildred Longbine, Connie Berry, Barbara Rickel, Fred Jarvis, Louis Truly, Evelyn Gugler, Marilyn Wolgemuth, Mildred Shank, Les Saulmon, Lola Smith, Eva Schnelle, Virgil Bennett, Charles Rickel, Shirley Baier, Earl Hess, Elmer Stroede, Charlie Widler, Edwin Schmidt, Helen Clegg, Robert Jamtgaard, Virginia Faulkner, Ethel Zeigler, Agnus Faulkner, Cheryl Soderland, Kay Hawks, Letha Correll, Edna Mae Emig, Dorothy Snider, Vesta Sidesinger, Pat Tyrell, Kathryn Brinker, Mary Bebermeyer, Ruth Lowman, Carl Wolgemuth, Pauline Strand, and Alice Hamilton.